# Table of Contents

# Introduction

This book is about starting and running a business successfully. It does not dwell on what type of business to start or why to start one. I suppose it is a filtered memoir. I was a technical salesman for many years and, much like a hairstylist, listened to the dreams and successes of innovators and risk takers. At the end of the book I've written what I call the "me, me" part, where I reveal why I am qualified to impart some of these ideas. Just a couple of points that might put this book in perspective: I have an honours degree in electrical engineering and I have an athletic mind—I know how to train and know what is required to race. In any kind of race, one is concerned with energy and its conservation. Can you momentarily rest on top of the hill or at the corner? Will the wind be in your favour? I am not sure whether the next statement is relevant, but I am sure it affects my outlook. I am an amateur musician and spend a lot of time thinking about music. I would be delighted to be a famous film composer as I'd probably die at an old age with all my faculties intact, and have lots of money.

This book does not include figures; there are other places for business statistics. I have avoided most clichés. The book is an insight into doing business, gained from talking to people who have successfully started businesses and those who have failed. I consider losing money, and even going bankrupt, to be failure—not when the business closes or is given away.

# The Thinking

I suggest you don't tell your relations or friends about your proposed business venture. What will it achieve? People will give advice, but some, who are jealous, will be pleased if you fail. If you need to talk over a business proposal, seek a mentor. Starting a business is different from running a business. The world is full of managers, and I suppose business schools do an adequate job of manufacturing them. Just remember that building a house is different from painting a house. It follows that starting tennis or chess clubs is different from managing them.

Two non-related observations haunt me: the perfect business model and top-seeded girl tennis players. Watch out for the perfect business model. It is great if you start one, like selling ice cream on a hot day at a busy intersection, or selling bottled water to tourists getting off the bus in Turkey just before their ninety-minute shade-free walk around Ephesus. Most girl tennis stars are tall. Often they are over six feet tall. Just name a few players you have heard of. Yes, there are exceptions. Yes, there are exceptions in business, and maybe your business is an exception and you may get away with it, but you should try to minimize the other problems. Your business will unlikely be a perfect business. Most likely it will be a marginal business, often on the edge. Even if you come up with a product called the telephone or the electrical light bulb, you will unlikely launch a successful business. Have you heard of Nikola Tesla? He was one of the pioneers of electrical engineering but few know his name. Guglielmo Marconi and George Westinghouse were also technically innovative, plus promotional.

## *Realistic goals*

You might start and successfully run a conglomerate and make bags of money, but it is unlikely. Your heroes might be Bill Gates, Sir Richard Branson, Sir Terence Matthews, and the many other business personalities—and there is nothing wrong with garnering positive attitudes and habits from these people—but remember that they are the exception. Let us be realistic. Your business is likely to be a marginal business for many years. If it ceases to exist, not too many people will worry. If you can create and run a business profitably and not go bankrupt financially or health-wise, then you have done amazingly well. So what is profitably? Can you earn as much or more from your own business than you could by working elsewhere? I have asked many business owners this question over the years. Here are some of the answers, none of which answer the question. .

"I like being my own boss."

"I can write off many of my expenses on the business."

"I can take an afternoon off to play golf when I choose."

"I tend to entertain business associates in restaurants."

"I don't have to spend money on business clothes."

"'I can pick up the children from school."

Often the conversation stalls before the admission that this business is a hobby business. As long as you don't fool yourself that the business is just that.

Now let us see if you are a good candidate for starting a business! Coming from a business family appears to help. That makes sense. However, professors of business, former vice-presidents of large organizations, civil servants over the age of 40, ex-military people, and of course MBA graduates are going to have problems. Surprised to read that MBA graduates have a difficult time? Ex-military people may still be young plus have funds, but their backgrounds have purged any business inclinations many missions ago. The problem with many of these people is that while they can successfully lead a team, implement plans and review projections, play other people's music well on the piano but are unable to write their own melody, are great in meetings, and have the business body language and talk, what they are missing is a burning desire. Passion. Well, also maybe ideas. Some people just want to be a business owner but are not sure what the business should be. We have all met people who tell us three times about a business they are going to start and the nature of the venture, but we are still none the wiser of what exactly they will be doing. This is not a good sign. Perhaps they should consider buying a business? I suggest you effectively learn to explain your business. Practise and rehearse this function so that you can do so between elevator stops. Do you know where your business cards are?

Don't be dismayed if you are not an ideal candidate to start a business. Just realize it. You can train to cycle up steep hills, but we all prefer to cycle on the flat.

Let us look at who tends to be successful? Immigrants are high on the list, as well as young people. Single women appear to be driven. I have often noticed that starters of businesses are not zealously academic but are passionate about what they are doing. They have a dream. So when is someone a business person and not a dreamer? It is a fine line!

# Preparing

This is where things can go wrong. It is one area that you will be visiting after you start your venture, so you might as well try to get it right. It is usual to write up a business plan, but go easy on the market research part, unless you are forming a market research company.

In the ideal world, your interest—or invention—blossoms, and one day you end up with a profitable company. That does not often happen! Perhaps you will start a business on the side. Moonlighting. Will it flourish so that you go full time? Your employer will not be too pleased if you spend time and energy on your side venture. Maybe if you are a pilot or a fireman then this can be easier. Many people understandably freeze before leaving the employer and striking out alone. Often it is one small issue that causes the jump, but it appears people are relieved when they go at it alone. Advice: try to leave your employer on good terms. There is immediate and exponential success with the full-time commitment.

The same is true with musicians and artists who become professional. Their craft improves, albeit their financial standing does not.

Starting a business for me is the same as preparing for a race. You train and get mentally ready. Yes, you can overtrain, and some people are perpetually preparing to start a business. In the end they prepare so much that they never launch the venture because they know it will fail. Usually they go on to teach at a business school. What!

## You need to get your finances in order

So start saving. Can you survive for about two years without pay, plus run a business? If not, there are problems looming. Of course, if you have a small fortune, this will not be a problem, at least not for a while. Getting a business going takes an enormous amount of time and energy. If you are involved in volunteer work, plan to phase yourself out. If you are big in sports and the arts, look toward changes in your lifestyle. Now, don't skip your fitness routine as your health is important. I think the last sentence should be written out once a week by all entrepreneurs. While we are in the life-skill mood, don't forget to review disability and liability insurance.

## What about business courses?

Take a few, but not too many. Bookkeeping, and maybe some on marketing and accountancy. I started an MBA and am glad I did not finish it. It was mostly course work appropriate for banks, government, and conglomerates that offer pharmaceuticals, personal care, or cleaning and pet supplies. What about courses on entrepreneurships? What about an afternoon workshop? That should be enough.

Entrepreneurship and innovation are trendy subjects to study, and they provide employment for business professors. These learned people justify their existence by highlighting the latest research studies on entrepreneurship and innovation. Often they are working on a new study themselves. Keep away from these people as you don't share the same beliefs. You have nothing in common. It is a bit like the high school rock guitarist and singer going to career counselling. The young musician knows he wants to be a rock star; the counsellor does not believe it. I am of the opinion that by the time you start a business, it is too late for business-type courses. For the first few months of my business, I studied philosophy at the University of British Columbia. Still with philosophy in mind, I discovered a collection of writings called *Management Secrets of the Grateful Dead*, which discusses strategic improvisation. This rock band was a master at business management. If you want to play music with Miles Davis, you had better know your chords. If you want to successfully start a business, then know your chords of the information technology. Make that smartphone sing. There are personal trainers for your body, and there are computer coaches. You may need both! My input here is to suggest you start your business as soon as you can and don't waste too much of your life gaining that invaluable experience. There is never a good time to start a business. Get in the water and start swimming. The more you learn about business, the more reasons for not starting one. But wait. I did say starting a business is similar to training for a race. I met a businessman recently whose enterprise never quite got going and he ended up merging with another company. He wished he had done all the mundane things associated with a start-up before jumping in. Matters such as name registration, business cards, books, and Web hosting—all valuable time drains. Remember, the race has started and your business has its own sundial.

## *Now what about where you reside?*

Are you living in an area that enhances the profile of your business? I am talking about a business that does commerce outside of its immediacy—those entrepreneurs who operate from a vacation town or in the hinterland of the back of nowhere. "Yes, but in these days of Internet, surely it doesn't matter where you reside?" Don't you believe it! Our prejudices have not changed that much. If you glance at the back covers of books, often you will read that the authors live for part of the year in some idyllic location, but for the rest of the time they are in London or New York. They want to stay connected. More people, more ideas.

## *Patents*

If your business has a new idea or service, then the subject of patents arises. In the past I would have said don't bother, it will take up too much time and money to obtain patents, and the large corporation will craftily cast you aside if it wants your idea. Today I am not sure. I suggest you seek advice.

# Partners

I have revisited this section many times and it is the section on which I have done the most work. I have even enlisted the advice of others but am in a quandary about the subject of partners. To ameliorate my problem, I do have a little fun in this section and have digressed a bit.

Listening to many people who have failed in business has made it clear to me that the universal theme is problems with partners. You could write the next few sentences.

"They wanted to expand too fast." "They lost interest in the business." "Personality problems." "Wanted to go in a direction that was not wise." "Started overspending."

Here is part of an e-mail from a successful business person who went through the partner trip:

"The partner thing, for me, was not ideal. We each had a different idea on growth, expansion, and development." I was told this business person was able to unbuckle themselves from the partnership without excessive grief.

"The first twenty-five years went well, but the last year was a nightmare, and I never want to go through that again." So said my cycling buddy after selling his business.

"My partner bought me out. We got along fine for ten years until I sold out. The process of selling out was terrible." So said another of my acquaintances. I have toned down what I would normally say about partners chiefly to not irk my readers. Most business people have partners, and my credibility would disintegrate if I were to dwell on the dangers of partners. It would be a put off for the rest of this book. Let us be realistic—if you already have partners, it makes no sense to dissociate yourself from them just because of a new Damascus conversion.

Here is a plot line:

Several people establish that they have a common interest and undertake a common venture or journey. One of the group becomes disillusioned and leaves the group. The remaining three others soldier on and eventually find treasure or the promised land. At first, one of them takes on the leadership role with consent, but later resentment, from the others. The leader warms to one of the group and gets him to kill the other. The leader finally kills off the last group member. The person who originally left the group shows up asking for some of the treasure or the land. The new leader treats the returnee with contempt. The returnee, after much argument, leaves with nothing.

It does sound like we have read versions of this before. I checked with my highbrow associates and they did not smirk, but concurred that the plot has traces of these tales:

The Greek mythologies with Jason and the Argonauts, or Agamemnon, Orestes, and Electra. It could be a Norse tale or part of the Finnish *The Kalevala*. How about the Norwegian Fortinbras? I understand Fortinbras was scheming all the time in the background while the Danes went through their family drama.

Maybe it was borrowed from Celtic mythology, as promulgated in the Welsh *Mabinogion*, which may not be on everyone's reading list. I was told that parts of the plot could have been lifted from the Jacobean play *The Travels of the Three English Brothers*. I warned you I was going to have fun.

It sounds like a good old biblical plot such as the one copied by Isaac and Jacob. Of course *Hamlet* must receive a mention, and we had better give a nod to *Macbeth*.

I composed that plot line after scanning the histories of several companies. The history of Facebook spurred me in this direction, along with that of Apple Inc. The former was founded by Mark Zuckerberg, Eduardo Saverin, Dustin Moskovitz, and Chris R. Hughes. Most of us know of Apple's Steve Jobs, and we technical types used to marvel at the "Woz," Steve Wozniak, partner of Steve Jobs, but the other founder, Ronald Wayne, is passed over. Bill Gates never has to say anything about his involvement with Microsoft, but Paul Allen, the co-founder, always has to remind us. I receive e-mails from Biz Stone of Twitter, and I see the other partners are all there—Jack Dorsey and Evan Williams. As I look at my Blackberry, I naturally think of Research in Motion—Jim Balsillie and Mike Lazaridis are well known, but have you heard of Douglas Fregin, who was the co-founder with Mike Lazaridis? Yes I know, these are successful companies.

Many of these partner stories appear amicable, but who really knows? What are the reasons for having partners? The classic one in my world is the engineer who needs to partner with a salesmen, or the salesmen who needs an engineer to make his gismo. The partner has the money. Well all right, the partner has the expertise. Do you really need this expertise? Can you not buy it when you need it? I have often seen the idea man partnering with an accountant. Usually not a good recipe. Think about it. How large does a company have to be for it to need a full-time accountant? What is he or she going to do in-between tax return time? Here are telltale signs of when potential partnerships are not needed: "Good to have someone to bounce ideas off," or when you are looking to make friends. Can you get out of the partnership without grief? Be aware of partnerships.

Mitel comes to mind. Terry Matthews and Michael Cowpland formed a successful company called Mitel, and then went solo on other ventures. So the best I can say about partnerships is to treat them as collaborations and be prepared for a life when the partnership ceases to be. Is no more!.

I see people embracing partners in the early stages of a venture for the wrong reasons. Try to do it alone. They could have launched the business on their own. I don't understand people openly starting a business and taking on partners when there is no

need. Think three times before having a partner.

# Marketing

I was going to skip this section and go straight to sales since it is the latter where most people have the problem, but marketing has a better ring to it than sales. You have collected countless business cards from marketing people who never want to talk or meet with a customer because they are busy doing another market survey that will result in a long-term strategic plan. Glancing at the "me, me" part at the end of this book, you will note that I completed a credit course of the MBA program, so I can write with impunity. By the time your business is off and running, you hopefully will have done your marketing: it is a hot day, you have found the busy crossroad, you have a supply of ice cream! I am not sure enrolling in a Marketing 101 course is much help if you have already launched the business. Your evenings might be better spent attending philosophy or woodworking classes. At least you won't get confused, and possibly you will have a coffee table on which to place those notes about St. Augustine.

Many marketing discussions take the form: total market size is X, and "if we only get two per cent of X, we will have a successful business." Now, it is all right to put this in your business plan and tout it at will, but I would be wary of believing too much in such talk when you are starting a business. This rationale emanates from the toothpaste/washing detergent companies such as Procter & Gamble. Most marketing seminars drill class participants in avoiding dependence on one or two customers—a philosophy that is sacramental in the MBA case-study world. So again I am knocking the MBA path—I did warn you. I am not refuting the wisdom of avoiding dependence on one or two customers, but I will add that from my experience it is exactly what happens. Many companies come into being because of one customer, and continue to survive and prosper because of one crucial customer. They may have many other customers, but it is the key costumer that permits the traces of arrogance to extol from its senior management. My comment is: live with it and make sure you don't upset your key customer, try not to let them know how important they are, and don't take too seriously all that MBA marketing stuff. I will re-mention Grateful Dead's concept of strategic business improvisation, but don't do it at the expense of the your key customer.

Many companies are killed by a single large order. It is hard to believe, but true. The reasons become apparent if you dwell on the situation. One might say, What a way to go? I don't have an answer to avoid this problem. Will you turn down such an opportunity? I am sure nothing I write will influence your decision, but I am saying be aware of the situation. Grateful Dead might suggest that you recognize the difference between a major and minor chord, and that you watch out for the dissonances.

## Sales

Sales is part of marketing, so if you are talking about sales, then you are ahead of many people. In the old days, the village supported one blacksmith. Not much need for promotion there. My engineering buddies believe that if they build a better mousetrap, customers will beat a path to their door. The word *mousetrap* is a euphemism for a new or better product or service. I have mentioned earlier that most businesses are marginal, and this mousetrap is likely to be only marginally better, so without sales we have a problem. Let us stay with my engineering buddies. Assuming they invent the first mousetrap, what they fail to grasp is that there is a large time gap between its introduction and sustainable sales. There must be books written on case histories of companies who failed to capitalize on first introductions. Examples of that come to mind: the iPad was not the first slate/tablet computer, but Apple's marketing catapulted it to the front. Educating the market is expensive.

What about advertising? It should be considered and of course does not have to be paid magazine or radio advertisement. It can be merely a flyer stating what you offer. Can the use of social networking sites derive you some business? Probably, so be conversant with them. Now, many people don't believe in sales. They might talk about sales but they don't believe. Let us be management-like here and see where we are and where we want to be. The first option is to do nothing, not even think, about sales. I will accept that doing nothing might be fine, as long as you know that is what you wish to do. Where do we aspire to be? No time for the customer's situation because you are busy filling an order for another customer. Then there is the "I am doing you a favour by attending to you," position—all right if you are the only ice cream vendor at a crossroad on a hot day! There is also idyllic and enviable word-of-mouth syndrome. Promotion is not needed in that case. I think I like the order-taking mentality, assuming you are inundated with orders. As long as you know which part of the salesmanship you are emulating, then everything is fine. Problems occur when you don't know what you are doing about sales …

I have a question. Are there more books on marketing than sales? I think so. But there are even more sales courses and seminars. So we like to write about marketing and not sales.

# What to Expect

## Income

You are not going to receive a paycheque. Yes, I have put that statement at the top. It is what makes you different. There is going to be enthusiasm for the first little while, and then loneliness. Maybe you will still go the gym at lunchtime and eat at the same deli? Maybe, but it is going to be difficult.

## Time management

It is likely you will be working long hours with little time off. You have heard that there are flexible hours when you run your own business. You get to choose which three hours you work after 6 p.m. You will realize that you can only see customers and suppliers during a finite number of business hours. Then there are the vacations. Well, not really. Maybe long weekends, and there is usually that week between Christmas and New Year.

People will look at you differently. Not sure what to make of you. Are you starting a business because you can't find a job? They try to justify the idea that it is better to not start a business, and recite reasons for not leaving their secure job. They will watch for signs of financial difficulties. Did you buy the ski pass? Are you still going to the local amateur theatre in the evening? Does the garden gate need replacing?

I canvassed some entrepreneurs about their problems. They talked about having to perform many functions—such as bookkeeping one minute and sales the next minute—many of which they did not enjoy. "I messed up on bookkeeping in my early months, but I learned."

One problem I had was socializing with people who did not place the same value on their leisure time as I did. I found this awkward as leisure time was important to me. These friends and acquaintances might have had a nodding interest in my venture but no understanding of the effort required. Why should they? Often they knew people who had had a business for a while. I found it difficult when out-of-town people came to stay. They did not understand the time pressure of starting and running a business.

Looking back, I see that I didn't develop new hobbies or become better in sports during that time. But I don't regret it. It was the price I paid. I did develop good work habits and managed to never become a workaholic, and the business was never my hobby. Time management was crucial.

Now lets dig deeper into some of the differences between working for a large company and a small one. Motivation and stimulation are important in both, but the large company has people and with people come ideas. So in your own company you have to compensate. You need those ideas as well as the stimulation thing—they will keep you from becoming isolated and then irreverent. I attended trade shows and lunches with business peers to keep me sharp. By so doing, I had to focus before the encounter, thus improving my outlook in a certain way. I often found the preparation more valuable than the encounter. Not unlike taking piano lessons. It is said that by taking piano lessons, one improves one's playing, even with a poor teacher.

# Creativity

Starting and running a business is a creative act. Painting a picture and composing music are also creative. But no one is creative for every moment of these endeavours. There is a lot of repetition with a business venture. Try to do much of your planning before you start, and practise the Grateful Dead philosophy of strategic improvisation as you go along. If you are an athlete, remember about pacing yourself. If you hit the wall, remember that you will eventually pass through it.

# Sales

I recently asked an entrepreneur what her problems were after a year in business. I was expecting many answers, including ones that I wouldn't understand. Her reply was immediate. "Sales." Her business is a new service in the real estate industry. She needs more sales but recognizes that she does not liking selling.

"I don't like rejection," she added. What she meant is that she was not making an effort to contact potential customers. This is very common. I happened to talk with an artist this week and asked if he had recently sold much? Yes, he had sold a painting the previous week, but he commented that he needed to spend more time on promotion. He liked painting but not sales. You have heard this before.

So let us look at sales. There is a megalomaniacal industry associated with teaching sales, but I think there is too much attention paid to this subject. It is necessary to promote your business so that potential customers can make a decision about doing business with you. So get organized and just do that. There are countless resources available for learning about promotion, and it is prudent to invest some time and energy in learning about the subject. In Greek Mythology, Hercules is sometimes marked as a supersalesman; also, Jason of Golden Fleece fame had a gift for closing the deal. Forget about mythological or so-called talented, super sales people. Let us look at ordinary sales people or even just ordinary people. Say you are a professional salesman. I was. What I did every day, five days a week, was sell electrical test equipment. Easy. That was all I did. One mindset. Do you know how to annoy professional sales people? Tell them they are merely order takers. I think your order-filling company is in an enviable position, but I think it is wise to keep the sales thrust going.

Maybe you don't like sales, but you want people to buy your services or your product. For small businesses, promotion is only part of what has to be done. The builder of fences wants to build fences; the electronic engineer wants to design new products. In music, when you change chords you are prone to making mistakes; in tennis, it's the same situation—moving to hit the ball is often an error. It is the changing of roles where most people have a problem, especially with sales, where rejection is common. The good news is that in small business, you don't have to be good in sales, only competent. You allocate a certain amount of time each day to the promotion of your business. Forget about all the stuff you have heard about closing and overcoming objections—just get out there and let potential customers know what you have to offer.

Don't be surprised if people don't act logically when it comes to buying. If you are not competent in sales, it means you are being rude. When I need a primer in salesmanship, I go into a shop and watch and listen to the sales associate. You will learn what you need to know and, of course, what you don't. Here are some tips:

- Try to find the correct person, the decision maker. You have to save your time and energy. You only have a certain amount of each.

- Always have business cards on you.

- Make notes in front of customers.

- Promptly respond to phone calls and e-mails.

- Be respectfully attired and groomed when you meet customers.

- Try to recognize the people who will never do business with you for whatever reason. They will waste your time.

- How many new contacts did you make this week?

- Did you follow up on all leads? A lead may be pivotal to the success of your venture, so treat them as money. You might want to watch David Mamet's film *Glengarry Glen Ross* to heighten the importance of a lead.

- Remember to sell yourself first, and then your product or service.

- Act like a salesperson.

- Attend specific trade shows and conferences. You can learn from competitors, so talk with them, but don't spend too much time, even if you feel they are a kindred spirit.

- Know when to stop selling, move on to the terms of the contract, and agree to a time frame of delivering product or providing service. When will you get paid? Some customers may only want to do business with you if they think they don't have to pay you soon or at all.

- Be aware if you are in the consultative or educating mode when pursuing opportunities. It may be necessary, but it is time consuming.

- If you don't feel comfortable asking for the order, don't, but I am sure you are curious whether there is interest?

- Follow up with the customer, but don't make that your goal in life. Your objective is to sell your product or service, not be a call centre for follow-up calls.

- Rejection is fine, and shows you are in the correct place.

- What about overcoming objections? How about not annoying the customer and listening?

- Customer is always right! Now, you don't believe that nonsense do you?

Here is a scenario to think about: you are not enthusiastic about promoting your service or product today. What if you had no product or service to sell! Often I have been in the waiting area of a company lobby with other salesmen and job applicants. It is clear from the body language of the receptionist and company escorts that they give less priority to the job seeker. Now, do you know where your business cards are?

# Getting Paid

Getting paid. This is the part of running a business that separates you from working for someone else. If you join a company, they will provide you with a paycheque for your services. If you are selling ice cream on a hot day, then you have a cash business, which has a lot of advantages. If you don't get paid, you eventually will go out of business, and worse, will owe money. I sent an invoice to businesses which I had performed a service for or shipped a product to, and I got paid within 30 days. Now, I have hobbies such as music, snowshoe running, and kayak racing but with some organizations, it is their hobby to avoid and delay paying suppliers. It is what they have always done. It is fun for them. They may have lots of cash on hand but they believe it is fair game to stall paying suppliers. Other companies and individuals are just irresponsible. It is difficult to know which is which, but the results for you are the same. The avoiding and delaying hobbyists will consume a lot of your energy, and hence reduce the profit on the transaction. I don't wish to provide a treatise on accounts payable or establishing credit—you can find that in other people's books. I suggest you dismiss any accountant's talk for a heading in the books about provision for bad debts.

A company founder's smiling face is on the front page of a trade magazine—revelling in the attention for garnering another business award or receiving patent number thirty-three. All very newsworthy, but be wary. Famous people often are not good payers. What about the company that has been awarded a large contract from a country that has an unpronounceable name? It doesn't mean they will have money to pay you. Another classic is the organization that receives a letter of intent from a government department to build ten garerangershusikers, with the option to increase the order by an additional six within fifteen months, as long as the price is kept firm. Just because the company is administered by Ben and Rogue Associates of Park Close, New York, with full membership to the Canadian Association of Insolvency and Restructuring Professionals, does not deter would-be suppliers from upgrading the organization to a key account status. I did write in the chapter on sales that:

"Some customers may only want to do business with you if they think they don't have to pay you soon or at all."

# Mistakes and Unforced Errors

I plan for this to be the shortest section. You probably could cite as many examples of companies being silly as I can. Do we enjoy recounting the errors of organizations? Maybe! I have learned that there is often a supposed reason for apparent stupidity. I remember a UK company turning down an order from Jerome & Francis Co. Ltd., a business I owned, because we no longer had a contract with them. No, they did not have a contract with another company, but they were following a policy. Try to avoid silly mistakes. Return phone calls and e-mail promptly. Don't start work on a project until you know that someone can and will pay you. Try to avoid silly mistakes—"Why did I do that?"—those unforced errors. Return to this page and try to keep it empty.

# Review Time

So when is review time? Tax-return time will jolt you into the land of the living, but we all know that reviews should have been done by then. I will add, don't underestimate the importance of tax-return time. Reviewing the preparation stages of the venture will be useful as most issues will be revealed. Chances are that things aren't going so well. So you are a marginal business. Well, I did point that out earlier. Maybe you can correct some mistakes and get another chance? Perhaps this is the time for a complete change in direction? Would the business be better doing something completely different? Grateful Dead would call it strategic improvisation—the ability to plan, act, and make adjustments in real time.

There are many scenarios. The common one is where the business appears to be doing well and making money but not a lot of money. Another one is where the business is doing poorly but there is a promise of a large contract that will change everything. Have you heard about the large order that killed the company? It happens.

Are passing the test of earning as much money as by being employed? How long do you keep going? A difficult and agonizing question. If the business is losing money how long do you wait it out before ceasing? Stop the bleeding, as investors might say. There is much assistance to guide you through this period. Let us keep in mind some common sense here and maybe some military strategy. You don't want to lose all your money and be completely defeated. You may want to regroup and fight another day. It is common for the owner to be working for a few dollars an hour. Hobby businesses or businesses for retirees are different. There are also those businesses run by rich wives. I think there is another kind of business called a vanity business.

Now, I wrote earlier that starting a business is different from running a business. If your business does well, adding someone to run things with a corporate shine will likely be in order. I didn't say take on partners. There are countless sagas of entrepreneurs who have messed up their own companies by not delegating.

The good news at review time is that there is always help available. It is easier to offer guidance to an existing enterprise than a vision. If you recall, I am not too keen about canvassing ideas. You have to do some things alone. Here is a snippet: if the business is apparently doing well, don't change anything. This might be harder than it sounds. Of course there will be bad days, but the business should be profitable. I also am postulating that you don't have to love what you do all the time—in fact the business might even do better if you don't enjoy every aspect.

For many business owners, review time is when they should examine their work pace. Do you have a good rhythm in your work habits? How will you keep yourself motivated? Have you visited your mentor recently? Who is your coach? What does the coach think? What training schedule is suggested? Do you need some interval training? Maybe two rest days a week?

# Epilogue

From its inception, a company or club assumes a certain culture. It may be a bad one or a good one, depending on how you view the world, but it rarely changes, even when new leaders take the helm. For example, there may be a strict dress code, formality, and an adherence to punctuality. There may be traits that are endearing when dealing with the organization, and others that are annoying. This culture has nothing to do with the success of the company and is hard to accept, as we only want the well-run, employee- and customer-considerate companies to be successful. Good and bad companies fail and succeed. The nasty company pontificates that it takes whatever action is necessary to be profitable, stay ahead of the competition, or stay in business. Remember, if you have ice cream on a hot sunny day at a crossroad, you can do whatever you like.

When I started this book, I derided MBA training as a starting ground for a business, but I now see an emergent body of thought questioning the usefulness of MBA methods for anything.

With the demise of Steve Jobs, we appear to be focusing more on his business philosophies than his innovative products, since his philosophies will outlast his products. In the antithesis of the MBA way, Steve Jobs did not believe in market research. Is Steve Jobs a good role model for you? Well, he does satisfy some of the conditions I pointed out early on, but remember, he was exceptional. You don't want to become dismayed if you are kilometres away from his shadow. I recently learned that he studied calligraphy and was a devotee of the Beatles and Bob Dylan. I find that interesting.

Is there a difference between mistakes and dangers? Dangers are situations that are difficult to prepare for. Mistakes are all those unforced errors. I did ask the advice of many people for this book. One successful business owner sent a dynamic e-mail which was helpful, but he had not started the company. He worked for the company first and then bought in. There is a difference.

One criticism of this book could be that I espouse mediocrity in starting a business. Not true. If you succeed in your own business, you are a success. There are not many of you.

I have reread the notes I made while writing this book and present them here:

- You should be able to effectively communicate in a few sentences what your business does. If you manufacture bows and arrows, then tell us.

- We all know about personal trainers and business coaches, but don't forget about information technology teachers. If your skills are drifting, you may need a few sessions.

- Your business's location is important.

- I believe businesses for retirees will be huge in the near future, and there still needs to be a new business model for them

- Don't forget about time—how to save time. Work on it.

- After a year or two, it might be prudent to change accountants.

I am still in a quandary about patents. Maybe try to get them, but don't spend too much money and time chasing them, unless of course your business is patent sitting.

Writing, publishing, and selling this book was similar to launching a new business. It was a new venture and follows the tenets for a new business. You might be asking if my advice is relevant, given that I come from a different business epoch. Has time moved on? It might be an interesting exercise to look for areas in the book that might be considered yesterday's, and are hampering the start and success of a venture.

During a flight to Turkey, I sat next to a forensic accountant who was travelling to a wedding. He worked for a large international accounting company. Telling him about this book was like joining a tutorial for vetting the book. He told me that he used to have plans to start his own business but that he no longer did because he was reluctant to forsake his financial well being. As a forensic accountant, he investigated many companies and saw similar traits. He told me the following:

- The difference between success and failure for organizations is marginal.

- Most companies are badly organized and do not know their actual costs. Sometimes they will sell at a loss because of pride.

- A company can be a nice company or a bad company and it has little to do with success.

- Getting paid is often a problem.

- Large companies take advantage of small companies. It is not always a good idea to do business with the famous companies.

He confirmed much of what I have presented.

# John Joyce BSc(Hons)

Well, this is the part that proclaims my credentials for writing a business book. I call it the "me, me" part. I started an electrical/electronic distribution business called Jerome & Francis Co. Ltd. thirty-four years ago. Two names, so immediately I appeared bigger than one person. I gave it a generic name in case the business went into different ventures, not necessarily electrical/electronic. I had been preparing to start the business for some time, especially the financial side. I bought a house before starting the business—yes, it's easier to get a mortgage when you are employed. I always made a point of canvassing the advice of business owners, though I am not sure I learned much, as often they were successful without knowing why.

When I started the business, I enrolled in an evening philosophy class at the University of British Columbia; too late for business courses, I thought. I believe I was correct. On my desk, I have a copy of Stephen King's *On Writing*. I find it motivational. So far I have read that Stephen King didn't rely on inspiration to produce works. He worked hard at his craft and apparently received a lot of rejection. What can I add to that?

When I was a little boy, I somehow heard it was best to have your own business. I recall someone saying you will never drive a Rolls-Royce working for someone else. There is a painting called *The Boyhood of Raleigh*, by John Everett Millais, on display at the Tate Britain in London. The painting depicts a young Sir Walter Raleigh and his brother listening to the exploits of a sailor. I see myself there, captivated by a future of travel and starting businesses. You are expecting a copy of the painting in this book, but you will only see several of my own paintings. You may buy prints! I was born at Hampton Court, in England, from Irish parents. Ah! the immigrant factor. Sir Walter Raleigh was vicious to the Irish, which I am not pleased about, and was beheaded, about which I am sure he was too pleased.

At Chiswick Polytechnic, the equivalent of a high school, I organized charity walks and school dances. While at Salford University, I travelled much of the UK with the cross-country club: I gained many ideas, especially about international travel. I proclaimed my intention to be an international technical salesman. I worked for the famous Marconi Company in Chelmsford, England— it is more famous now because of its historical association with the birth of radio and for the fact it no longer exists. The first day there I told them I wanted to be in sales, but I was sent to the corner bench and told to design a Butterworth filter which was needed in a new UHF television transmitter for the BBC. I made a point of having a one-on-one meeting with a senior salesman of the division. I didn't learn anything, and looking back, realize he was an order taker for Marconi. He had worked for Marconi all his career, and sales was a promotion for him. Perhaps if the Marconi Company had hired technical salesmen they would have survived? I recall I was always interested in meeting the salesmen that visited the company, and attended trade shows at any opportunity. What a tiresome employee! I am grateful to the Marconi Company for hiring me. In my business ventures, I have always delegated clerical and office matters as soon as possible, which is a trait I learned at the Marconi Company.

I moved to Canada for adventure and joined a sales company that sold electrical and electronic test equipment. I had found my perfect job. The company was well run, and individuals were given a lot of responsibility. The company was not cheap, and I was grateful for what I learned. I knew I was destined to start my own company, so off I went. I received a lot of assistance from the founder of the company for which I am grateful, and I am still in contact with him. Business managers have choices when an employee openly says he wants to start a business. It might be construed as competition, but with me , it was taken as a compliment that they had hired someone gutsy enough to go into business. Maybe the nagging doubts that they had hired the wrong person were dispelled. While the new business, Jerome & Francis Co. Ltd., was taking shape, I started a lawn-cutting business. It was quickly successful, and for several months it paid the mortgage.

I learned many things from the lawn-cutting business: how dependant I was on staff, and how fortunate I was when they stayed. I learned about the power of advertising to recruit staff and to obtain new work. As Jerome & Francis Co. grew, so my interest in the lawn-cutting business declined. Often I had to cut the lawns myself when there was no staff, and I objected to the time incursions. You can start and run a business for which you have little interest, but in the end you need the interest. The business died out. Why didn't I try to sell the business? It is very difficult to sell a business, and time consuming. I think I handled matters well by concentrating on my venture. I try to stay focused, and as with tennis, woodwork, and romance, try not to make mistakes.

Now you are expecting me to mention my regrets with my business dealings. Well, I won't, since I am not finished yet. I still have some business ideas but they tend to be hobbies. So, can you make money out of your hobby?

I spend time organizing sporting activities. The discipline is good and I enjoy the different people I meet. I also feel I am putting back.

Have you learned anything new about business from this book? Perhaps some points you had forgotten about?

Maybe it has prompted you to think about issues that I have passed over. So, ice cream on a hot day sounds good to me. I know a crossroad where …

Follow me on Twitter there:  http://twitter.com/altusarts